The Basic Essentials of
COOKING
IN THE OUTDOORS

by Cliff Jacobson

**Illustrations by
Cliff Moen**

ICS BOOKS, INC.
Merrillville, Indiana

THE BASIC ESSENTIALS OF COOKING IN THE OUTDOORS
Copyright © 1989 by Cliff Jacobson

10 9 8 7 6 5 4 3

Printed in U.S.A.

Published by:
ICS Books, Inc.
One Tower Plaza
107 E. 89th Avenue
Merrillville, IN 46410

DEDICATION

To my loving wife Sharon, who prefers the luxury of her kitchen to the adventure of cooking in the wilds.

Library of Congress Cataloging-in-Publication Data

Jacobson, Cliff.
    Cooking in the outdoors : the basic essentials of / by Cliff Jacobson ; illustrations by Cliff Moen.
        p.   cm. -- (The Basic essentials series)
    Includes index.
    ISBN O-934802-46-7 : $4.95
    1. Outdoor cookery.   I. Title.
TX823.J33   1989
641.5'78--dc20
                                                            89-35056
                                                            CIP

TABLE OF CONTENTS

Figure 1-1   "Foods that work to keep you working!"

1. FOODS THAT WORK
TO KEEP YOU WORKING

Whenever I return from one of my lengthy canoe trips in the Canadian wilds, someone invariably broaches the subject of foods. What kind and how much do I bring? How do I pack crushables like eggs, crackers and breads, so they won't be mashed inside heavy packsacks? Are there inexpensive plastic containers that won't leak after a month on the trail? On a long trip, fresh foods are out. And except for special occasions, so are cans. How then, do I accommodate variety and good taste? A steady diet of oatmeal, peanut butter, and "Hamburger Helper," may be nutritious enough, but it doesn't inspire excitement.

Then, there's the not-so-simple matter of preparing foods in the field. Whipping up a gourmet meal in a major downpour calls for procedural skills that you won't find in cookbooks.

In the heat of discussion, someone always brings up the subject of "nutrition." That a food tastes good, looks appetizing and provides plenty of energy for a strenuous outing isn't good enough. This individual wants to know how the nutritional value of each entree compares with "U.S. Recommended Daily Allowances."

That a balanced diet is as important in the woods as at home, is a forgone fact. But how scientific do you have to be when planning an outdoor cuisine? Not very — as long as you apply

1

common sense and don't rely too much on a few good things. What works at home will work in the wilds — with one exception: calories! You need lots of 'em — 4,000 or more per day if you're really working hard. By comparison, a typical homemaker expends about 1,400 calories a day, an office worker about 2,500; a factory worker approximately 3,000 calories.*

An average hunter, hiker, or canoeist, will burn about five calories per minute (300 per hour, 2,400 per eight-hour day); a cross-country skier, biker, moutaineer or backpacker, may use twice that amount. Keep in mind the obvious fact that extra work requires extra fuel, provide an assortment of foods from which to choose, and you'll have no problems with nutritional components or complaints. However, if you must pursue a scientific course, just remember that a pound of body fat contains about 3,500 calories. With this knowledge, plus a calorie/nutrition chart (available in every foods text), you can easily plan meals that will retain your body weight and keep everyone happy.

Fortunately, you don't need to be too scientific in determining "nutritional value", as your body's natural craving for variety will help you make sound food choices. Simply know to which food group each edible belongs (fats, carbohydrates, proteins), and "weigh" your daily food intake so it corresponds roughly to the following formula:

CARBOHYDRATES

Carbohydrates provide quick energy and should supply at least 50 percent of your daily requirement — easy enough, for these are everyone's favorite food group. Breads, cereals, honey (honey and tea is the traditional north country drink), jam, dehydrated fruits, cookies and candy, are rich in carbohydrates.

FAT

Fats contain over twice as many calories per pound as carbohydrates and are the body's major source of stored energy. They

---

*From *Biology of Work*, by O. G. Edholm, McGraw Hill, 1967.

also carry the fat soluble vitamins — A, D, E, and K. Generally speaking, fats should provide about one-fifth of your daily intake of calories, though for a really tough trip that amount should be increased substantially. Except in calorie- burning winter, when you might go as high as 40 percent*, 25 percent is a good ball-park figure.

Admittedly, it's hard to carry a lot of high fat foods on a back country trip without significantly increasing pack weight and bulk. Examples of food which contain fats are margarine (I prefer Parkay liquid), cooking oil, nuts and peanut butter, cheese, bacon and sausage.

Because fats aren't converted to energy as fast as the other food groups, they allow us to go without eating for long periods of time. Verlen Kruger, who amazed the world by paddling his solo canoe 28,000 miles in three years, once commented that his favorite food was pancakes, smothered with margarine (a primary fat source). Verlen said he could travel "five miles per pancake!"

PROTEIN
The typical 160 pound adult needs about 45 grams (1.6 ounces) of useable protein per day. But for traveling the backcountry, you'll need much more. A hearty breakfast of oat or wheat cereal and reconstituted dry milk; a lunch which includes cheese, beef jerky, peanut butter or sausage; and a supper which contains dehydrated or freeze-dried meat (or if you're really enterprising, fresh fish) will provide all the protein you need.

Note: proteins are not stored to any great extent in the body, so those eaten in excess of energy and tissue repair requirements will be converted to glycogen and stored as fat. For this reason, it's best to space protein intake throughout the day, rather than to ingest it at a single sitting. Moreover, if your calorie count is insufficient for the activity and there are no carbohydrates or fats available to supply energy, the proteins you eat will be converted directly to glucose (energy). For this reason, you're wise to combine

---

*You need more oxygen to metabolize fats than carbohydrates or proteins. For this reason, fat intake should be reduced when working at high altitudes (above 12,000 feet).

some other high energy food with your protein snack to get full
nutrition from it.

VITAMINS AND MINERALS

It's only on extended (several months) trips that you need to
be concerned about vitamins and minerals. Even then, don't worry,
as a balanced diet invariably contains everything you need. Only
the water soluble vitamins (the B and C group) must be replenished
regularly. And that's no problem if you supplement your meals
with vitamin C fortified fruit drinks, jams, dehydrated fruits, and
vitamin B-rich cereals. Incidentally, high doses of vitamin B com-
plex make you smell bad to mosquitoes — that's something to
remember when traveling in bug-infested country.

FOODS THAT WORK

Freeze-dried and dehydrated foods: Dried foods have made
the wilderness life much easier. The best ones taste as good or
better than canned fare but are lighter and more compact. And if
you stick with supermarket entrees, they are also quite inexpensive.

Nonetheless, canned goods (*please* carry out the cans!), in
limited amounts, are a welcome addition on most wilderness trips.
After days of reconstituted dried fare, canned peaches or pears,
chilled in a nearby stream, are divine nectar. And so is an occasional
meal which includes canned bacon, green chilies (on scrambled
eggs) or spaghetti made with genuine tomato paste. The sage advice
that "cans have no place on a wilderness trip" applies only to
strenuous backpacking ventures where every ounce counts. If you
want to produce varied, delicious meals *at low cost*, you'll need
to rely on some select canned goods.

Freeze-dried foods: Fresh or cooked foods are flash frozen and
placed in a vacuum which draws off about 98 percent of the moisture
by evaporating the ice at temperatures of - 50°F. or so. The freeze-
dried food is then sealed in moisture and oxygen-proof packaging.
Shelf life is virtually unlimited. The freeze-dried product maintains

full nutrition and nearly full flavor. And the food retains its original shape and texture. The stuff looks as good as it tastes.

The problem with freeze-drying is that it is very expensive. A three ounce serving of FD hamburger or chicken costs around three dollars! A meal of beef stroganoff, chili or spaghetti (14-ounce serving) may run $3.50 per person, and this doesn't include much meat.

Dehydration: Scores of books have been written about dehydration, and I'll leave the details to them. I do a fair amount of food drying and can heartily recommend the EQUI-FLOW model 7010 (Equi-Flow Dehydrators, Inc., 4403 Russell Rd., Lynnwood, WA 98036) dehydrator for those who are really serious about efficient food drying.

However, dehydration must be a labor of love. It's slow, messy, and it requires lots of food preparation time. You can dehydrate anything, though the reconstituted flavor seldom matches fresh, canned, or freeze-dried products. You'll save about 50 percent over co-op purchased dried foods, and toil many hours in the kitchen. Whether the time commitment is worth the money you'll save, depends on your perspective.

Each summer, I guide canoe trips into the wilds of Canada for the Science Museum of Minnesota, commonly with groups of ten. With three exceptions (hamburger, chicken, and some sauces, which provide the basis of dozens of trail meals) the time required to dehydrate a week's supply of food for a group this large simply isn't worth the effort. And I've come to this conclusion after being well practiced with a top line dehydrator.

Tip: You don't need a commercial dehydrator to dry foods. Your oven will work, albeit inefficiently. Meats are best dried at a temperature of around 140°F. If your oven thermostat won't go that low (check temperature with a food thermometer), you'll need to use an auxiliary heat source. In her book, "Supermarket Backpacker", Harriet Barker suggests substituting a 150 watt light bulb for the standard oven light, as your *heat source.* Oven racks are covered with cheese cloth and the product to be dried is placed on top. If you're doing hamburger (meat should always be as lean as possible) place several sheets of thick paper toweling on a cookie sheet and set the fried, *well drained* (put the meat in a strainer and pour boiling water over it*) hamburger on the toweling. Prop open the oven door slightly so moisture can escape. Rotate the tray frequently to ensure even drying.

My own experiments with oven drying have been "marginally" satisfactory. Often, the food has a "cooked" taste (the result of too much heat), the reason why I bought a commercial unit.

Figure 1-2
A muscle-bound Popeye
slugging down "moose juice."

*Boiling water will leach some nutrients from the meat.

As important as dried foods are to the success of a backcountry outing, they alone don't supply enough energy to keep bodies humming happily. As mentioned, you need lots of calories on a tough trip and that means extra amounts of breadstuffs, peanut butter, margarine, nuts, cereals and cheese. Important in all wilderness foods is that they be lightweight, slow to spoil, easy to prepare and stable in hot weather. These requirements alone necessarily eliminate many otherwise excellent products from your shopping list.

You'll also want to know which foods *really* work to keep you working and which don't. And you won't find that information on a calorie chart or from nutritionists who don't camp. That's because a food can look good on paper and be completely worthless on the trail. A good example is "Moose Juice."

Moose Juice was a product of the mind of Verlen Kruger and the 1966 Atikoken, Ontario to Ely, Minnesota canoe race. The Atikoken to Ely run was once touted as the toughest canoe race on the continent. And with good reason. Equipped with only the bare essentials of a canoe, map and compass, rain gear and food, competitors would paddle non-stop to Ely 55 miles away. After a rest, they'd run back again at top speed. The 100 mile route included 28 grueling portages, several huge lakes and an occasional bog. Navigating in the dark called for a high degree of resourcefulness; most canoe teams never finished the race; many canoeists became lost. (Evidently, the Ely to Atikoken race ultimately proved too tough as it has since been discontinued for lack of competitors.)

To supply his body with the energy necessary to maintain the quickened 60 stroke per minute cadence used in canoe racing, Verlen developed a "complete nutritional liquid supplement" which he affectionately named "Moose Juice." When Clint Waddell, Verlen's partner, learned of the nutrient concoction, he objected strongly. But Verlen, a soft-spoken man of infinite patience, pointed out that Moose Juice was a product of modern science. It met every nutritional requirement, didn't need to be unwrapped or cooked, and could be consumed on the run.

Clint wasn't convinced so he hid away a few sticks of beef jerky "just in case." Good thing, too: "Just in case came about four hours into the race when Clint became violently ill from the effects of the home-made brew. The beef jerky helped some, but not enough. In the end, the Moose Juice won and Clint and Verlen lost the race.

That episode points out an obvious but often ignored food fact: *the physical makeup of foods must not be so unusual that they disagree with your system*! And since one person's system rejects what another's relishes, you'd best stay away from fancy or unusual edibles until you've first tried them under fire — that is, the fire of your own kitchen stove.

You may also find that your body dislikes "sameness" in foods. A continuous diet of oatmeal, dried milk, dehydrated fruit and peanut butter may be scientifically acceptable fare, but your stomach may refuse it anyway. No need to prepare gourmet delights to please your system, but you may want to give it a few simple food options to choose from.

The old Northwest Company did a lot of research on foods during the fur trade days of the 17th and 18th centuries. They found that pemmican* was the only food which a man could tolerate for long periods of time. Even today, pemmican is considered an excellent trail food, though most wilderness travelers never learn to develop a taste for it.

Okay, enough about nutrition and food hokum. Time now to check out specific foods and the methods for preparing them.

---

*Seventeenth century pemmican usually consisted of pressed buffalo meat with a generous amount of buffalo grease added. The voyageurs often mixed the pemmican with flour and water and cooked up a substantial soup called "rubbaboo," which they heartily devoured daily for weeks at a time.

2. THE KITCHEN

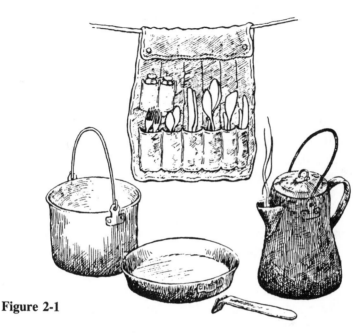

Figure 2-1

You can't do good work without good tools. Badly designed, flimsy cookware won't do. Unfortunately, most pots and pans you buy for camping fall into that very category. For a party of four, you'll need the following gear:

*Three nesting pots with covers.** The largest pot should have a 16 cup capacity so you can cook pasta without gluing it to the bottom.

Tip: Engrave lines on the pot sides at two cup intervals and write the total capacity (e.g. 16 cups) just below the rim. This forethought will eliminate guesswork and the need for measuring cups at meal time.

*Pots may be aluminum, stainless steel, or porcelain-lined carbon steel. Sustained cooking in aluminum has been linked to Alzheimer disease — hardly a concern considering the minimal use received by camp cookware. Where weight and bulk is a primary concern, the kit can be reduced to two pots and a light skillet. Some backpackers travel with only a single pot! Best cookware is made by Sigg of Switzerland and Mirro of the United States.

For faster and more even heating, you may want to blacken your pot bottoms. A few sessions over a campfire will do it and so will *Alumablack* — a chemical agent used for darkening aluminum gun parts. Similar to "cold blue," every gun shop has it.

One relatively straight-sided, 10-inch diameter, Teflon- lined skillet.

Avoid flimsy teflon-lined pans with folding handles that are sold in camping shops. These warp and flake after a short time. You'll find the best skillets at your local discount store.

Remove the stock frying pan handle and use an aluminum "pot gripper" (the heavy-duty "genuine Boy Scout" model is by far the best). Or install a captive screw and a removable handle.

Eight cup coffee pot or kettle. A wide-based kettle heats faster and is less tippy than a coffee pot, and you can pour with one hand. Pack onions, green peppers, cheese and other crushable/breakables inside your empty kettle.

An oven of some sort: either a wide ring Jello mold (for baking on a stove), a shallow, broad-based pot and cover for use as a "Dutch oven," or an extra skillet to function as a "triple-pan" oven. See Chapter 6, *The Art of Baking*, for the details of using this gear.

One or two stainless-steel Sierra cups, for use as compact ladles and emergency cups, and for stewing fruit in your Jello mold oven (Chapter 6 shows you how).

One nesting plastic bowl per person. Bowls should be color-coded so each person always uses the same one. This will eliminate sharing germs at each meal.

Keep the nested cook-kit/oven and bowls inside a generously fitted nylon sack.

Fabric utensil roll: You can make or buy one. Be sure it has snaps or ties on top so you can hang it from a clothesline. Chapter 7 details the rationale.

If you want to go light, one metal spoon per person is enough. Gourmet cooks will add a fork. Everyone carries their own knife and insulated plastic cup (mug). A wood-handled, rubber spatula doubles as a stirring and mixing spoon, pot scraper, and frosting spreader.

A wire-whip is essential for reconstituting dried soups and mixes.

These items should all fit nicely in your utensil roll.

Don't forget plastic containers for spices, liquids and flowables: See Chapter 7 for what works best.

Salt and pepper shakers: 35 mm film cans are ideal. Get protective salt/pepper flip-tops at any camping shop.

Two-quart graduated plastic pitcher: Convenient for mixing powdered drinks, pancake mixes and instant puddings, and for hauling water to the cooking site.

Dish washing materials: A four ounce bottle of liquid detergent, a plastic sponge and abrasive 3-M nylon scratcher is all you need for trips up to a month long.

One *thin-bladed* sheath knife with a four to five inch long blade. Try to spread jam, scrape peanut butter from the bottom of a poly bottle, or slice lunch meat or cheese with a common jack knife and you'll see why a long-bladed knife is so important! In case you're wondering, my favorite trail knife is a Gerber Shorty.

Gasoline stove: Ideally, you should have one burner for every four people. Of course you can cook on a fire (where permitted), but weather frequently makes this impractical.

3. BREAKFASTS TO BEGIN THE DAY

Figure 3-1

Some years ago, while guiding eight teenagers on a canoe trip in Ontario, I came upon a young couple whose tent was pitched flat dab in the middle of the portage trail. It was early morning, and the day was punctuated by a cold, persistent rain. We'd begun our travel at 3 a.m. in the calm of night, hoping to beat the stopper headwinds which usually arise with the sun.

Our traveling fuel for the past five hours had been two Carnation Breakfast bars apiece and a couple of beef sticks. The kids were famished. And chilled. We'd agreed to stop at the portage (the only flat spot around), build a fire, and cook a wholesome breakfast.

Within minutes after landing, colleague Al Todnem and I had a cheery blaze going and a double rain-tarp strung overhead. Al put the finishing touches on the fly, while I fired up the two Optimus 111B stoves and began frying bacon. This accomplished, I turned my attention to the "mocoa" (a mixture of coffee and cocoa: kids love it!). The fire was burning nicely, so I set the light stainless grill across two logs and put on the 20 cup kettle. "Maybe 20 minutes," I mused. "By then, everything will be done."

Back to the stoves to give the bacon a stir. Pour off some grease, consolidate the meat into the big skillet. Add a cover to keep in heat. turn down the flame to simmer.

"How you want your eggs, Angie?"

"Over light," comes the reply.

In a second, skillet two* is wiped free of grease with paper toweling packed with the breakfast meal. A teaspoon of vegetable oil is added, and the eggs go on. Again, a cover speeds cooking. As the eggs simmer, I check the bacon, then slice a bagel and put each half face down next to the eggs. I salt and pepper the eggs, cover 'em, and relax with a cup of just brewed mocoa.

Two sips later, the eggs are done. I shovel them into a bowl, squirt the bagel halves with Parkay, and direct Angie to the bacon.

"Next! How ya want your eggs, Tom?"

Total preparation time for this meal — ten people — is just 35 minutes. Add another 30 to build and extinguish the fire, warm cold feet, do the dishes and burn the trash, and we're out in just over an hour.

Warm and well fed? You bet!

Oh yeah, about that couple in the tent. Mid-way through our meal they struggled, bleary-eyed into the chilling drizzle, marveled at our set-up and politely asked if they could warm up by the fire. Then they retired to the vestibule of their tent where they awkwardly heated a small pot of water on their Peak I stove. For breakfast they had tea and instant oatmeal, which they consumed in cold Sierra cups beneath the dripping umbrella of a white pine tree.

---

*You need one skillet for every five people. Or, you can bring a grill that spans two stoves. Skillets/grills should be Teflon (or similar substance) coated, *carbon* steel, or stainless with copper bottom. Pure aluminum is an abomination unless it is *very* thick.

They were still sipping tea and looking into the sky for salvation as we trucked down the portage trail. They were ordinary Fords and Chevys; we were the sports cars that just blew past!

As you can see, outdoor cooking is a whole lot more than "menus." Even simple meals are not at all easy to make when the wilderness becomes competitive. Here are my favorite meals to start the day, along with tips for preparing them:

SLOW COOK MEALS

Requires boiling, frying, or simmering. Maximum preparation time for four people is 20 minutes. You'll need one good trail stove or a well-tended fire, plus the "kitchen" suggested in Chapter 2.

BACON/EGGS/BUTTERED BAGEL WITH JAM

Bacon: Sliced, sodium-nitrite rich store-bought bacon will keep at least three days in July heat. Slab (unsliced) bacon may last a week or more. I've kept vacuum-sealed Canadian bacon for ten days. Mold won't grow without air, the reason why vacuum-sealing works so well. Most large grocery stores have vacuum-sealing machines and will wrap your meats accordingly, and at no extra charge, if you request.

For very long trips, try *Celebrity* canned bacon (a product of Hungary). It is lower priced than supermarket bacon and it has less fat. Shelf life is unlimited.

Eggs: Dried eggs are available at every camp shop and co-op. Some supermarkets have them. You can even get cholesterol- free dried egg substitutes at supermarket delicatessens. But hype aside, none can compare to fresh eggs.

Supermarket eggs may be several days old when you get them. Even so, they'll usually keep unrefrigerated for at least a week in hot weather. Farm fresh eggs will last two weeks or more, that is, if the shells remain intact. Never break eggs into a bottle for easy

---

*I've had excellent results vacuum-sealing my own foods on a machine called the FOODSAVER, available from Nationwide Marketing, Inc., 2415 Third St., Suite 235, San Francisco, CA 94107. Phone: 1-800-225-0647. Cost, at this writing, is about $250.

carrying: once the bacterial barrier (egg shell) is destroyed, they'll spoil immediately.

How to carry fresh eggs: Small and *medium* sized eggs have thicker shells than large size and so are less apt to break in transit. Carry eggs in molded-plastic cartons (available at camping shops), or pack them in coffee cans, cardboard milk cartons, or your tea kettle, cushioned with popcorn or wads of paper toweling.

Bagels: I prefer "Lender's" raisin bagels for breakfast. The raisins prevent the bagels from drying out, thus increasing unrefrigerated pack life to a full week. Double bag bagels in plastic or, for real longevity, ask your grocer to vacuum seal them. Bagels are nearly indestructible. Left-overs can double as frisbees.

Cooking Procedure

At home, you'd separate bacon strips, lay them flat and cook them slowly, with plenty of "breathing space." In the woods, you need a more efficient method, especially when you must prepare a lot of bacon for a large crew. Fire up the stove (medium heat) and add bacon all-at-once to a *cold* pan. Swish it around at the start to get some grease distributed, then immediately cover the pan. Stir the tangled mess frequently. Pour off grease only if it threatens to overflow the pan. The combined deep-fry/cover-steam process will cook 1-2 pounds of bacon to lightly crisp perfection in less than ten minutes.

To keep cooked bacon hot until you're ready to eat, place it in a covered pot lined with paper toweling and snug your down vest over the pot (as "tea cozy," if you will). Or place the meat in an inverted pot lid lined with toweling, set atop a pot of near boiling tea or dish water. Heat from the hot water below will keep the bacon toasty warm.

Eggs: Wipe the bacon skillet clean of grease and bacon scraps before you begin the eggs. Yes, you can cook eggs in bacon grease, but you'll probably burn them. Better to use a clean pan and fresh vegetable oil. A teaspoon of oil is needed even in a Teflon pan. The skillet should be *moderately* hot.

If your stove puts out too much heat at its lowest setting, use a flame-spreader (a tin can lid works great) between the fire and pan. A pan cover is essential, especially on a windy day.

I cannot overstress the importance of using fitted covers on all your pots. Low temperatures and a chilling breeze can rob enough heat from cookware to prevent uniform cooking.

Bagels: Slice a bagel, slide the almost cooked eggs to the edge of the skillet and place each bagel-half face down in the steaming pan. Cover for 20 seconds, then remove eggs and bagel from the pan. Note that everything's cooked to perfection and is ready to serve *at the same time.*

PITA MELT AND EGG McPITA

Here's a fast-cooking breakfast that's always a hit. You'll need one pita (mediterranean pocket) bread per person, 2-3 slices of Canadian or regular bacon and a slab of good cheese. Plastic-bagged pita bread (at most supermarkets and all Greek foods stores) keeps at least two weeks in summer. *Hard* cheese like Cheddar or Colby may last a month. Just trim away any surface mold that appears.

Preparation procedure: Fry the bacon and set it aside. Leave a hint of bacon grease in the skillet. Place a pita bread into the *low heat* skillet, top with cheese and bacon and cover. When the cheese has melted (about 30 seconds), the meal is done.

Fold the pita bread over, sandwich style, and serve. You can also make an "egg McPita" by adding an "over-medium" fried egg to the sandwich. You may substitute summer sausage, ham or salami for the bacon.

LUXURIOUS PANCAKES

It's pointless to make pancakes or muffins from scratch when so many good mixes are available. Just use Bisquick or your favorite batter and these tricks of the trade:

1. Disregard the mixing directions. Pour the dry mix into your two-quart plastic pitcher and add water, a little at a time, stirring frequently, until the consistency is *moderately runny.* The

tendency is towards a too thick mix which cooks badly in the field. Batter will thicken as it sets; you'll have to thin it again later.

2.   Add about two tablespoons (the amount isn't critical) of melted margarine to each six cups of liquid batter. The margarine will make the cakes more flexible and less likely to stick to the pan.

Figure 3-2   "Frisbee the first pancake away!"

3.   Use *medium* heat and just *a few drops* of cooking oil to fry the first half dozen cakes. It's par for the course to frisbee the first cake into the fire to get the skillet heat right. Don't attempt Mt. Everest by frying several cakes at a time. Instead, limit your accomplishments to *one cake per pan.* Keep each cake *thin* and spread it nearly to the skillet edges. Again, a cover speeds cooking.

After the first half dozen pancakes, you can limit use of cooking oil to a few drops every three cakes or so. The margarine in the mix will provide the lubrication you need.

4. Completed cakes are kept hot in a covered pot set near the stove, or use the down vest/tea cozy arrangement explained earlier.

Meanwhile ... pour your cold syrup into a small covered pot and add 50 percent margarine and a dash of cinnamon (optional). Heat to near boiling and set aside. Pancakes will later be smothered with this hot mixture.

Further ideas: Try peanut butter as a topping. Sounds awful, but adds a wondrously rich taste. For a gourmet touch, add a handful of cooked wild rice to the mix. Oh m'God, this is incredible!

Let's review the tricks: 1) Batter should be pea-soup-thin. 2) Margarine adds taste to the mix and all but eliminates burning. 3) One cake per pan is the rule. 4) Flamboyantly discard the first cake as a matter-of-fact! 5) Heat syrup and mix half-and-half with margarine.

BRANDY-STEWED FRUIT

Ingredients: One package of mixed evaporated fruit, ¼ tsp. cinnamon, 2 heaping teaspoons of white or brown sugar or honey (you can substitute sugared cherry or apple - flavored drink crystals), 1 shot of brandy, Yukon Jack or Southern Comfort.

Cooking procedure: Place fruit, sugar, cinnamon and whiskey and enough water to cover the fruit into a small pot with tight-fitting cover. Bring to a boil and simmer for 15 minutes or until fruit is tender. The result will excite the stodgiest crew. Note: you can save considerable preparation time by steaming everything in a Jello-mold oven as explained in Chapter 6.

CAMP OMELET

Ingredients: Eggs and cheese; onion and/or green pepper (optional).

Cooking procedure: Beat the eggs and pour a *thin* layer into a hot, greased skillet. Salt and pepper to taste, add diced onion and/or green pepper and lay thin slices of cheese on top. Cover immediately and cook on low heat for about a minute. then, flip half the egg over to sandwich the cheese and veggies inside. Cover and cook another half minute or so. Optional: top with spicy salsa or Cajun hot sauce.

QUICK COOK MEALS

Requires boiling water and perhaps a few minutes of simmering.

INSTANT OATMEAL, CREAM-OF-WHEAT, RALSTON, MALT-O-MEAL

I allow two packs per person. "Maple and brown sugar" flavor is most popular. Add raisins (a must!) and milk or non-dairy creamer. When instant cereals become old hat, try mixing them: Maple/brown sugar oatmeal with apple/cinnamon cream-of-wheat, etc. Add fruit bits or sugared dates for a pleasant change.

RED RIVER CEREAL WITH STEWED FRUIT

This distinctive Canadian cereal is the pride of fly-in fishing camps all over Canada. It's crunchier than oatmeal and it cooks in just five minutes. Prepare it according to directions but add raisins or stewed fruit to the cereal *at the start* of cooking. A topping of milk, brown sugar and margarine is essential. You're gonna love it!

HOT GRANOLA CEREAL

Ingredients: Any cold granola breakfast cereal, Milkman Instant Milk*, raisins or sugared dates.

*MILKMAN is instant low-fat dry milk with a kiss of cream. It reconstitutes easily with cold water and a taste that's hard to distinguish from fresh milk. Each 8-ounce glass contains 90 calories. One package makes 32 ounces. Costs about a dollar per quart from Indiana Camp Supply, P.O. Box 211, Hobart, IN 46342. Indiana Camp carries a complete assortment of dried foods. Free catalog.

Preparation: Just add boiling water, fruit and Milkman mix all-at-once. Cinnamon and a dollop of honey adds spice to what is already "very good stuff!"

EASY TOAST

Set a *dry* (no cooking oil) skillet on a medium-hot stove or fire. Sprinkle about one-fourth teaspoon salt into the skillet and set your bread or bagel-half on top. The bread will toast to a golden brown without burning, and the salt won't stick to the bread.

TASTY CAMP BEVERAGES
COFFEE, SPICED COFFEES, MOCOA, MOCOA-MINT

Use fresh, *fine ground* coffee. Bring water to a boil then *remove the pot from the heat.* Add one tablespoon coffee per cup to the pot. Stir once, cover the pot and *set it aside* for about three minutes. Some cooks add a dash of cold water to settle the grounds, but this is unnecessary and simply cools the brew.

Tips: For gourmet coffee try adding a quarter teaspoon cinnamon and/or a splash of almond extract to eight cups of coffee water.

To make "mocoa," use instant cocoa mix and substitute brewed coffee for the hot water. "Mocoa-mint" flavor results when you add a few drops of peppermint extract to the coffee/cocoa mix. For an interesting alternative, try a splash of peppermint schnapps in your mocoa.

Some cooks add a light pinch of salt and an egg shell to the coffee water. The key to making great camp coffee is to *boil only the water,* not the coffee!

4. MID-DAY REPAST

For most Americans, lunch, per se, is more traditional than essential. In the wilderness, however, it is both a time to fuel the body and soothe its aches and senses. Hiking boots are shuffled off and "hot spots" are curiously attended; sweltering brows are wiped with cool, clear water; bodies yawn out full frame for a moment's doze. For the next thirty minutes or so, there is time to relax and appreciate the incredulity of God-made things.

Given your present state-of-mind, the very last thing you want is to toil over a cranky stove, nurse a reluctant fire, or cook up a gourmet meal and afterwards wash and dry the dishes.

Simply put, lunch should be easy. If you can't unwrap it, slice it, spread it, or open a can, forget it. On a really severe day you might cheat and boil some water for tea or instant soup, but basically, you'll bring a cold bag lunch — one prepared back home under the auspices of sound nutrition and good taste.

Hikers, bikers, canoeists, hunters and fishermen will all choose from these time-proven entrees:

21

Figure 4-1   "Mid-day Repast."

Pita Bread: Same stuff you used for the "Pita-melt" in the last chapter. Pita is my main-stay bread for nearly every noon repast. One pita per person is plenty, even on a gut- wrenching high altitude hike. Stuff your pocket bread with:

Block cheddar or colby cheese. Avoid "soft" and sliced cheeses of any kind; these spoil quickly. Processed cheeses (which aren't really cheeses at all) are tasteless and oily. Remember, mold won't grow without air — reason enough to specify vacuum-sealing or a full wax covering.

Sausage or salami which needs no refrigeration. "Barrel O'Beef" Cervelat and Summer Sausage keep for weeks in summer heat if the casing is not broken. Figure one-eighth pound per person per meal.

Peanut butter

Jam or jelly: Kraft jellies in the rugged, "squeezable" plastic containers are convenient.

Other lunch ideas

Bagels: Raisin and onion varieties stay fresh longest (about five days).

Granola bars, Crunchola bars, Carnation Breakfast Bars, Kudos, etc. and any candy that melts in your mouth, not in your hands.

Wylers/Kool-Aid instant drink mixes.

Mixed evaporated fruit, fruit bits or sugared dates.

Fruit breads (Banana, pumpkin, or date-and-nut: I use a pre-pared mix.) Or try the wonderful Hudson Bay Bread and North-woods soda bread described on the next page.

MONSTER COOKIES — a meal in itself.
Ingredients
3 eggs
1 cup white sugar
1½ cups brown sugar
¼ tablespoon Karo syrup
2 teaspoons baking soda
¾ teaspoon vanilla

¼ pound margarine
¾ pound peanut butter
Shelled, salted peanuts (add what you like)
4½ cups oatmeal
½ pound M & M's
Preparation: Mix in bowl. Drop on to greased cookie sheet (flatten the tops) and bake at 350° for 12 minutes. Makes about two dozen gigantic cookies.

HUDSON'S BAY BREAD: Another complete meal, Hudson's Bay Bread is traditional traveling fare in youth camps from Maine to Minnesota and throughout Canada. This age old recipe is as delicious as it is nutritious.
Ingredients
2 cups white sugar
2 cups margarine
½ cup light Karo syrup
9½ cups rolled oats
    Mix together ... 1 cup sliced almonds
Optional: 1 cup coconut, chocolate chips or raisins, as you prefer. Or mix these to suit your fancy.
    Preparation: Stir the almonds and coconut into the other well-mixed ingredients. Spread a half inch thickness of the mixture on to a greased pan and bake at 350°F. for about 18 minutes or until golden brown. Cut into bars. Makes a five day supply for a crew of four.

    GORP: An anachronism for "good old raisins and peanuts;" there are many variations. Here's my favorite (add or subtract what you like):
Ingredients
    Mix approximately equal amounts of M & M's, raisins, blanched, salted peanuts (not dry-roasted), salted, shelled sunflower seeds and Cheerios. Spice the concoction with a handful of chopped sugared dates. Great shelf life ... and taste!
    Note: You'll find dozens of recipes for heavy breads and "bars" in conventional cookbooks. Simply select what strikes your fancy, and *don't* take the recipe too seriously. You really don't need every

ingredient on the list. Even the amounts can be shuffled within reasonable limits. If you don't have "whole wheat flour," substitute white enriched flour. No coconut? Leave it out. And yes, you can make delicious breads, cakes and biscuits without milk or eggs. Recipes are a guide to good eating, no more. Discover this, and you'll be well on your way to becoming an excellent camp cook.

5. HYACINTHS FOR THE SOUL

After a fast-paced breakfast and determined lunch, supper is hyacinths for the soul. At last there's time to stretch out before a crackling fire and savor a tasty meal and second cup of coffee without concern for self-imposed time constraints or the ambitions of your friends. And later, if hunger tugs an ambitious cord, there's corn to pop, brownies or cakes to bake and flavored teas or hot spiced liquor.

The mealtime gathering embodies all that's right and good about being in a place that's wild and free.

A grand (which need not mean lavish) supper encapsulates the mood of the day and sets a favorable tone for the morrow. A slovenly, tasteless meal evokes the opposite. Fortunately, quality suppers are easy if you adopt these guidelines and proven tricks.

RECIPES

As stated in the previous chapter, recipes should not be taken literally. Seldom do you need every item, in the amounts indicated. Cakes, for example, usually call for eggs — something you can omit on the trail and not miss at all. White sugar can be substituted for brown; or use honey, Karo, or maple syrup. In a pinch, try

Figure 5-1   "Don't be afraid to experiment."

flavored, sweetened drink crystals. Need to stretch a meat/rice or pasta dish? Just add some instant soup, potato buds or Bisquick dumplings to the mix. And don't be afraid to mix flavors: i.e., chicken-vegetable soup and beef stew. Imagination, and a willingness to experiment is the key to successful trail meals.

SPICES
The blandest trail meal becomes King's fare when artfully spiced. In addition to the expected salt and pepper, I carry celery

flake, dried green peppers, onions, lemon pepper, Cajun seasoning, and my own "all spice" which consists of approximately equal amounts of the following ingredients:

Seasoned salt (I buy a commercial blend)
Oregano
Marjoram
Dash of thyme
Dash of onion powder

Mix the above ingredients and pack them inside a 35 mm film container.

PREPARATIONS

Field rations usually contain three basic parts: pasta or rice, meat or TVP (textured vegetable protein), and veggies. Need more food value in a given meal? Just add elbow macaroni, noodles, Minute Rice or cheese. Stretch vegetable components with dried soups or mixed vegetables. Add dehydrated hamburger to stews, soups and rice and pasta dishes. Or throw in diced, fried sausage, canned shrimp or crab, or chunk-white chicken. Here again, creativity pays rich dividends.

The *veggi-cheese* soup exemplifies the principle:

VEGGI-CHEESE SOUP (serves 4)
Ingredients

Lipton's or Knorr Instant vegetable-beef soup (double the suggested package servings to yield 8 servings)

1 lb. (fresh weight) of dehydrated hamburger, or substitute ½ lb. of diced/fried summer sausage or two 5 oz. cans of chunk-white chicken. For another alternative, try chicken-vegetable soup with chunk-white chicken or shrimp.

2 inch cube of cheese
Handful of wide egg-noodles per serving
A dash of your special "all-spice"

Preparations: Make the soup according to package directions but add *20 percent more water.* Add dehydrated or canned meats and spices at the start of cooking. When water boils, throw in the egg noodles. Simmer about five minutes or until noodles are tender, then cut the cheese into thin wafers and add it to the stew just before serving. Delicious! And, a complete meal in itself.

Dumpling Soup is another easy trail meal based on the same principle:

DUMPLING SOUP (serves 4)
Ingredients

Instant Minestrone, vegetable, beef-vegetable or chicken soup (double suggested serving amounts to yield 8 servings)

⅔ cup of uncooked Minute Rice

⅔ cup of Bisquick

Optional: Handful of dehydrated hamburger or a half-cup of chipped/dried beef. If you're using a chicken soup base, supplement with 1 can of chunk-white chicken or a package of freeze-dried chicken.

Pinch of your secret all-spice.

Preparations: Add 20 percent more water than called for in the directions. Failure to do this will produce glue, not stew! Add meats and spices to the cold water. Bring to a boil, add Minute Rice, then drop marble-sized dumplings into the brew. Simmer about five minutes, until dumplings are done. Here again, you can add cheese at the last moment or beef up with fried sausage or canned meats.

Tips

To make dumplings (or biscuits) without soiling your hands, pour batter and water into a plastic Zip-Lock bag. Seal the bag and knead the contents with your hands until they are well mixed. When the consistency is correct, punch a hole in the bag bottom and squeeze the mix — use the bag like a cake decorator — into the soup (or your oven).

Gourmet Award is the best tasting chicken soup base I've found. Use it like bouillon; no refrigeration necessary.

Matzo Meal is a flour used to make unleavened matzos — a popular flat cracker that looks like "hem-stitched cardboard." It's available at Jewish delicatessens and most supermarkets.

Traditional "matzo-ball" (dumpling) soup is easily made in the field by adding one onion, a dash of celery flake, and a hint of tomato (if you have it) to one ounce of soup base for each five cups of boiling water. Drop golf-ball sized matzo balls into the brew; add a handful of wide egg noodles (optional), and you have a 20 minute treat that you'll relish at home. For a pleasant change, try matzo meal in other soups too.

Fried matzos is another unique dish that's easy to make in the field. Just dip slabs of matzos into a salt and peppered beaten egg mixture and fry until golden brown. Top with syrup or brown sugar. Matzos is inexpensive and it keeps for months on the trail.

CHOWDERS

Chowders are tasty and easy to make. This recipe, suggested by my friend, Bob Dannert, serves 4-6.

Dehydrated hashbrown potatoes: 3 cups.

Potato Buds: enough to make two quarts of cooked potatoes.

1 fresh onion, or substitute one-fourth cup of dehydrated flakes.

1 T green pepper flakes.

Handful of dried mushrooms (optional)

Handful of dried corn, peas or other vegetables — be imaginative.

Three packs (each pack makes one quart) of Milkman instant milk mix.

Fresh caught fish or substitute canned shrimp or crab.

Preparation: Place everything except Potato Buds and fish into your largest pot. Add sufficient water to rehydrate the mix and to make a slushy soup. Bring to a boil, stirring frequently, then add enough Potato Buds to thicken the brew to the consistency you like. Or, thin with water, as you prefer. Salt and pepper to taste.

When the chowder is cooked, add one-inch chunks of raw fish to the lightly boiling brew. Cook five full minutes (to kill any tapeworm parasites), no more, and serve immediately. Makes around 12 cups.

Tip: For a great taste treat, add raw fish chunks (5 minute boil) to any instant soup mix.

Figure 5-2   "For a great taste treat add raw fish to any soup mix."

CLASSY SPAGHETTI (Serves 3-4)

First rate spaghetti is a class act in the wilderness, and it's easy to make. Here's my recipe:

Ingredients

1 packet of Schilling (or other) Spaghetti sauce.

1 small onion (or 1 T of minced, dried onion) will suffice for up to 8 servings.

½ small, green pepper. Or substitute ½ t dried flakes.

A dash of dried celery flake.

1-6 oz. can of tomato paste. Note: tomato paste (and prepared spaghetti sauce) may be reduced to an easily rehydrated "leather" in any food dehydrator.

A dash of your "all spice."

Vermicelli (cooks faster than regular spaghetti). I use one pound for each 4-5 people.

Dehydrated hamburger: one-fourth pound per person. Or, substitute fried, diced summer sausage, salami, Canadian bacon, or canned ham. All these meats work well.

1 small can of mushrooms (dried mushrooms are very good) for each 4-10 people.

Dash of coarsely-ground red pepper.

1 T Parmesan cheese per serving.

2 T margarine.

Preparation: Fill your largest pot with water, add a dash of salt and a cover; heat, and turn your attention to making the sauce.

Place sauce ingredients, spices, meat, coarsely cut vegetables and margarine, plus three cups of cold water (more or less, as you like) into your medium pot. Bring to a boil, stirring frequently. Simmer five minutes, while stirring constantly, then set the pot (covered, of course) near the fire to retain heat as you turn your attention to making the pasta.

Add *full length* Vermicelli to the now boiling salt water and cook until "endente" (slightly tough). Serve immediately. Top Vermicelli with sauce and Parmesan cheese.

Tricks of the trade: Making spaghetti with full length strands is a class act. To prevent breakage in transit, carry uncooked Vermicelli in cardboard tubes (those from rolls of paper toweling are ideal).

Note: Camp spaghetti sauce is best made too thin rather than too thick. Thick sauces burn easily under the concentrated heat of a trail stove, even when stirred constantly. Always add at least 25 percent more water than recommended.

If you're short on stove fuel, don't waste it cooking pasta. Instead, bring Vermicelli to a boil, cook for one minute, then set the covered pot aside (preferably, near the fire) for 15 minutes. The retained heat will cook the noodles.

Don't attempt to drain pasta water. A predictable mess invariably results. Instead, pluck noodles from the pot with a fork.

Place a few teaspoons of cooking oil or margarine into the pasta water to keep the noodles from sticking.

For totally classless spaghetti, break up the Vermicelli and cook everything in one pot. The mush that results will be unimpressive but tasty.

SUPER CHILI FOR FOUR

Of all bush meals, "classy spaghetti" and "super chili" are the hands down favorites. Chili made with dried components is edibly presentable, but when a few canned ingredients are added, it becomes downright mouthwatering. There is no right or wrong way to make chili. Vary components and water amounts to suit your fancy. It's almost impossible to ruin chili!

Ingredients

1 pkg. of Schilling chili seasoning mix — mild, medium or hot, as you prefer.

1-6 oz. can of tomato paste. For decidedly inferior chili, substitute four envelopes of Lipton's tomato Cup-A-Soup for the entire tomato component.

1-8 oz. can of tomato sauce ... or double the tomato paste ... or use one 15 oz. can of tomato sauce.

1 coarsely chopped fresh onion.

1 coarsely cut green pepper, or a teaspoon of dried pepper flakes.

1-16 oz. can of kidney or chili beans ... or use equivalent weight cooked, dried beans.

1 lb. of fresh or dehydrated hamburger. Or use diced, fried summer sausage, Canadian bacon, canned ham, or TVP.

1 cup elbow macaroni or spaghetti broken into 2 inch lengths.

Salt and pepper to taste, plus, a shot of your "all spice."

Ground red pepper (optional).

Preparation: Throw everything, *except the macaroni*, into your largest pot along with 3-½ cups water (use 4 cups if you're using the all tomato paste recipe). Bring to a boil, then add the macaroni. Simmer ten minutes, stirring constantly. Cover and set near the fire for ten minutes, so retained heat will cook pasta. Stir before serving. Top with ground red pepper and/or small chunks of cheddar cheese.

NORTHWOODS STIR-FRY (serves 4)

Scenario: First night on a wilderness campout. You want to wow your friends with a gourmet supper of grilled filet-mignon, rice topped with fried mushrooms and gravy, and a fresh salad. (See Chapter 7 for the logistics of carrying fresh fruits and vegetables.) Problem is, the weather won't cooperate. Rain is coming in sheets and everyone has miserably retired to their tents.

Everyone but you, that is. Your mission is to fulfill your promise to feed the crew a luscious meal.

At the outset, you'll have to rig a rainfly to get out of the weather. My books, *Camping Secrets* and *Basic Essentials of Camping*, will show you how. However, even with overhead protection, grilling steaks in a determined rain is at best, awkward, and frying them is the ruination of good meat. The answer is to forget about campfires for now, and instead concentrate on making "northwoods stir-fry" on your stove. The ingredients at hand include:

4 mouth-watering 8 oz. tenderloin fillet's

1 head of lettuce

1 tomato
1 green pepper
1 fresh onion
1 can of mushrooms
2¼ cups of Minute Rice
Cooking oil
Small plastic bottle of salad dressing

Procedure: Place a friend in charge of making the salad. He/she gets the lettuce and tomato only. You keep the rest. To eliminate dirtying a pot, make the salad in a plastic poly bag. Add dressing and shake.

Fire up your stove(s). First, put on the teapot and prepare a round of "Hot Buttered Yukon Jack" (recipe follows) to brighten up the crew. In this chilling rain, a "hot toddy" served with a twinkling smile will establish your expertise as camp cook.

Meanwhile ... Slice steak, pepper and onion into bite-sized strips and pile them in a small pot. This accomplished, put on the water for Minute Rice. If you have just one stove, you'll need to shuttle pots as follows:

1.   Teapot goes on first — requires about 10 minutes to boil.

2.   Remove hot teapot: your assistant serves "hot Jack" while you put on water for Minute Rice — about 8 minutes to boil.

3.   Remove boiled Minute Rice water, add rice and set the covered pot aside. If the weather is cold, cover the pot with your sweater or down vest to keep contents hot.

4.   Pour a few tablespoons of cooking oil into the skillet, warm it slightly, then toss in the meat, stirring frequently as you fry. When meat is half done, add the vegetables and mushrooms. Salt and pepper to taste and saute until everything is done (8-10 minutes). Serve *over* a bed of rice (inept cooks will mix everything together) with a salad side dish.

As soon as the main meal is off the stove, re-fill the teapot and put it on again, this time to make cinnamon or amaretto coffee (recipe is in chapter 3), which will be done ten minutes later.

Eat and enjoy ... and laugh at the weather. Your total preparation time is about 30 minutes.

HOOVER CURRY (serves 4)

Named for the Hoover Wilderness Area in the Sierras, this scrumptious recipe was refined by Mickey McBride, a whitewater canoeing fanatic and ardent mountain roamer.

1 T of Curry powder
1 pinch of red pepper
1 t dry minced garlic
¼ cup dried onion flakes
2 cups of Minute Rice
1 pkg. of Knorr leek soup mix
3-4 oz. of golden raisins
1-5 oz. can of chunk-white chicken, or 1 pkg. freeze-dried chicken.

Preparation: Combine all ingredients but the chicken in a Zip-Lock bag at home (if using FD chicken, it's best to add 2 teaspoons of dry chicken broth to the mix). To prepare, bring 5 cups water to boil, stir in ingredients and simmer 10 minutes, stirring occasionally. If sticking occurs, add a little more water. Serve with freeze-dried peaches.

For more than 4 people, or for a gourmet touch, serve with Knorr Hot and Sour soup.

CAMP TODDY'S

After a tough day afield, the traditional hot toddy hits the spot. It can be prepared with any whiskey or liquor, though Yukon Jack, Southern Comfort and Pusser's rum tastes best.

Combine the following ingredients in an insulated mug:

1 shot of whiskey
1 t sugar
Dash of cinnamon
Pat of margarine
Add boiling water and stir

Superb! Try substituting hot apple-flavored Kool-Aid or cinnamon tea for the boiling water.

Let's review what we've learned about preparing suppers in the outdoors:

1.   Don't take recipes too seriously. More or less — or omission of — selected ingredients will seldom spoil the stew.

2.   You can substitute similar foods for one another without seriously affecting flavor.

3.   Increase nutritional value of meals by adding Minute Rice, pasta, instant mashed potatoes, or soups.

4.   Use spices willingly.

5.   Don't believe the "servings" information on the package. The average adult needs around 14 ounces of cooked food per meal (more, in strenuous conditions) to retain body weight. I *always* double "suggested servings" amounts.

6.   Don't be afraid to experiment.

CAJUN COOKING

Yes, you can have genuine Cajun meals in the bush. Packets of gumbo and jambalaya come complete with seasoning and rice and are available by mail from these companies:

Tony Chachere's Creole Foods
P.O. Box 1687
533 N. Lombard St.
Opelousas, LA 70571-1687
Phone: 800-551-9066

Oak Grove Smokehouse
17618 Old Jefferson Hwy.
Prairieville, LA 70769
Phone: 504-673-6857

Gumbo and jambalaya cook up in 20 minutes. Add the recommended amount of water; include an onion, tomato and green pepper, and a can or three of shrimp or crab, plus a generous dash of Tony Chachere's famous Creole Seasoning, and you'll have fare fit for a king.

6. THE ART OF BAKING

Used to be, only seasoned woodsmen who understood the nuance of yeast breads and well-regulated campfires could prepare mouth-watering baked goods in the outdoors. Everyone else just watched in awe, content to eat their high energy crackers and whatever they could boil on their gasoline stoves.

Now, advancements in foods technology (there's an instant mix for everything) and cookware have made it possible for anyone to produce perfect cakes and biscuits every time. All you need is a prepared mix, a source of flame (stove or fire), and one of the commercial or jury-rigged ovens suggested below. Here's the procedure:

BAKING ON AN OPEN FIRE
Reflector Oven Method
Baked goods are set on the well-greased shelf of the oven, which is placed before a *roaring* fire. The key here is *roaring*, as the bright aluminum reflector needs high flames for even heating of upper and lower surfaces. If you can't maintain a hot bright fire, forget about using this appliance!

Figure 6-1   Reflector oven baking is easy.

Reflector ovens were popular a half century ago when large campfires were the norm. Today, small fires — or no fires — are the rule, so the bulky reflector is out-of-place. Nonetheless, reflector baking is easy and fun. And because your food is always visible (not hidden in an enclosed oven), you can take immediate action to prevent burning before it occurs.

Procedure: Set the oven about eight inches away from the roaring flames. You may have to elevate the fire base (on rocks or logs) slightly to ensure even heating. Baking times are about the same as your home oven.

You'll need a *long-handled* metal spatula to shuffle the buns during the baking process, and a can of "Bon-Ami" to keep the aluminum surfaces bright. When not in use, fold your oven flat and store it in a protective fabric bag. Where can you get a reflector oven? Try camping shops or your local Boy Scout supply center.

Figure 6-2   Baking a bannock.

Baking in a Skillet — The Traditional Bannock

A bannock is a bread which is baked before an open fire in a large straight-sided skillet. It can be as simple or complicated as you like. I usually start with a *stiff* Bisquick dough, then add whatever's on hand — raisins, dehydrated fruit, cinnamon, sugar, honey, or "all of the above." Fold in what you like, in the amount you like.

Baking procedure: Spread the dough, about an inch thick, right to the edges of a well-greased frying pan. Then, set the skillet on ash-covered coals (avoid flame) for a few minutes and *slowly* cook the bottom of the bannock, occasionally shuffling the pan to prevent burning.

When the bottom of the bannock is golden-brown, build the fire high and prop the frying pan about 45 degrees to the leaping flames. Occasionally rotate the skillet (or bannock) until the entire surface of the bread turns a delectable golden brown. Test for doneness with a sliver of wood shaved with your pocket knife. Add a topping of honey and margarine and you'll consume the bannock in one sitting, ashes and all!

Figure 6-3   "Woody's" dutch oven.

Dutch Oven Cookery

The aluminum or stainless steel "dutch oven" in which you prepare stews and soups at home, is a far cry from the proud artifact which bears the name. A *genuine* dutch oven is made of pure three-sixteenth's inch thick or heavier, cast iron or aluminum. Several short legs at the base keep hot coals from touching the pot bottom, and a rimmed (deep dish) cover supports a glowing fire on top. In a traditional dutch oven, you can bake, boil or fry with equal aplomb.

Your best source of old fashioned, round dutch ovens is a Boy Scout supply center or a mail order catalog that caters to horse wranglers and big game hunters. Cast iron ovens cook best, but they are terribly heavy and awkward to carry. Aluminum models, though lighter, are just as bulky. One light-weight unit which bakes well and packs compactly is the "Woody" dutch oven. Made of three-sixteenth inch cast aluminum, two sizes are offered: 6½ inches by 9 inches (3 pounds), and 9 inches by 9 inches (6 pounds). Each oven section may be used separately as a griddle. These high quality units are available by mail from Indiana Camp Supply, Inc., P.O. Box 211, Hobart, IN 46342.

Using the dutch oven: A new cast iron oven must be "seasoned" to prevent sticking and burning of foodstuffs. The recommended method is to coat the pot with cooking oil then place it, sans food, in a 350°F. oven for an hour or so (same as breaking in a cast iron skillet). Or you can eliminate this folderol and use the oven as is, knowing full well that your first efforts will be imperfect. Aluminum dutch ovens do not need to be seasoned to prevent sticking or burning.

A well-seasoned oven needs very little grease. A few drops of cooking oil, evenly spread with paper toweling, is enough. Place dough in the oven bottom — a two inch thickness is about right. Cover the unit and set it over, but not touching, hot coals. *Tip:* if your dutch oven does not have legs, cover the coals with ashes to insulate them from the pot bottom. Fill the depression in the oven cover with glistening coals, or build a hot fire on top. Occasionally turn the oven and rotate the cover to ensure even heating. Since the vast majority of heat is applied to the oven *top*, there's little chance of burning the bread inside.

Figure 6-4
"You can make a dutch oven from any pot and lid."

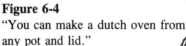

Note: You can easily make an acceptable dutch oven by inverting a large frying pan over a smaller one, or by placing a skillet, cake pan, or inverted cover on top of a pot. However, the thin aluminum construction of this makeshift appliance suggests that you use almost no heat on the bottom (set the oven in the warm ashes). A small, hot fire on top should provide nearly all the heat for baking.

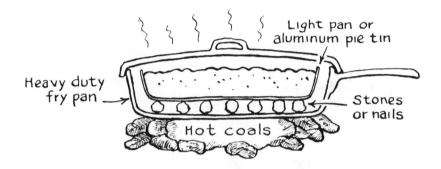

Figure 6-5   Triple-pan method of baking.

BAKING ON A TRAIL STOVE
The Triple-Pan Method
You'll need two nesting skillets (or one skillet and an aluminum pie tin), a high cover, and a half dozen small nails or stones.

1.   Evenly scatter the nails or stones onto the bottom surface of the large skillet.

2.   Place your bread or biscuits into the small frying pan or pie tin and set it on top of the nails (the air space which separates the two pans will prevent burning).

3.   Cover the unit and place it on your stove. Use the lowest possible heat setting.

Warning: Don't use a thin aluminum pan on the bottom: you'll burn a hole right through it!

Tip: you can use the triple-pan oven over an open fire too!

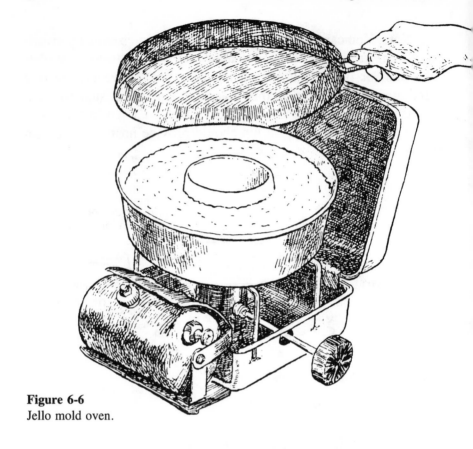

Figure 6-6
Jello mold oven.

Jello mold Oven

All you need is a large ring aluminum Jello mold (about three dollars at most discount stores) and a high cover. To use the Jello mold for baking on your stove:

1.   Grease the mold and pour your bake stuff into the outside ring. Decrease the suggested amount of water by up to 25 percent for faster baking.

2.   Bring the stove to its normal operating temperature then reduce the heat to the lowest possible blue-flame setting. Center the Jello mold over the burner head, top it with a *high* cover (essential to provide room for the bread to rise) and relax. Heat goes up through the chimney of the mold, radiates off the cover, and cooks from the top, with no chance of burning.

3.   Cool the mold by setting it in a shallow pan of water for a few moments.

Important: Even a light breeze will cause uneven heating of the Jello mold, resulting in a cake that has one side burned and one side raw. So rotate the mold frequently to distribute heat evenly. A windshield of some sort is essential when using a Jello mold oven.

Other Uses of the Jello Mold

As a steamer: Steam will rehydrate your dried fruits and vegetables much faster than boiling water. The procedure is simple.

1.   Fill a stainless-steel Sierra cup two-thirds full of water and set it in the chimney of the Jello mold.

2.   Space the fruit or vegetables evenly around the mold.

3.   Cover the mold and turn your stove on high. Steam will build quickly as the water in the Sierra cup boils. Your fruit will rehydrate in about five minutes.

Note: If you don't have a Sierra cup, place the mold in a *shallow* pan of water. Pour water into the pan through the hole in the center of the Jello ring. You want just enough water to cover the bottom of the pan without floating the mold. Add your fruit or veggies as before; cover, and apply heat.

Baking With Sterno

Scenario: You're camping in an area where fires aren't permitted. You'd like to bake some biscuits but your stove is tied up making supper. How can you utilize your Jello mold oven?

Easy. fire the Jello mold with a *small* (2⅝ oz.) can of Sterno (don't use the large can: it puts out too much heat!).

Place the can in the center of the ring mold and cover the oven. The Sterno needs oxygen to burn so you must ventilate the mold by raising it slightly (prop it on a pair of half-inch diameter sticks). Ventilate the oven cover by cracking it about one eighth of an inch.

An advantage of Sterno is its reliability in wind. With the mold propped only one-half inch off the ground, there's little chance the flame will blow out. The safety and reliability of canned heat make this oven a natural for use inside a tent or at high altitudes.

Other Uses of the Jello Mold Oven

There are times when you want to fix a single cup of cocoa or tea, but the wire pot supports on your trail stove are too far apart to stabilize your steel Sierra cup. The ring mold will provide the sturdy base you need.

Place the mold on the stove with the ring centered over the burner and set your Sierra cup in the chimney. If you want faster cooking with less heat, add a cover.

RECIPES

Earlier, I suggested that it's hard to beat the prepared mixes available at your supermarket. There are two exceptions: "Northwoods soda bread," and genuine sourdough. Here are the "working" recipes.

NORTHWOODS SODA BREAD

This is one of the best trail breads around. One slice is a complete meal.

Ingredients:

4 cups flour
1 t baking soda
1 T baking powder
¾ t salt
2 T sugar
1¼ cups of raisins or chopped sugared dates
1 beaten egg
1 cup of buttermilk or sour milk (milk can be soured by adding 1 T vinegar or lemon juice per cup of milk).
1 cup unflavored yogurt or sour cream.

Preparation: Knead it all and bake at medium heat (350°F. in your home oven) for about an hour. Note: This bread is easily made in the field by substituting dried sour cream for the real thing, and vinegar-soured Milkman drink mix for the buttermilk. The basic recipe is foolproof: I've substituted brown sugar for white, added jam and cinnamon to the mix, eliminated the eggs and used reconstituted non-fat dry milk instead of yogurt. It is always excellent!

Traditional Sourdough

Making the starter: Into a stoneware crock or plastic bucket with tight-fitting lid, put about two cups of flour, one tablespoon sugar, and one-half cake of fresh yeast. Add enough warm water to make a medium-thick batter. Let the mixture set at room temperature about three days until it "sours," after which — unless you plan to use the sourdough every day or two — store it in the refrigerator to slow working of the dough.

To make bread or biscuits, remove about one cup of well-stirred liquid and place it in a mixing bowl. Replace the batter you took with a small amount of flour and fresh water. Add about one- fourth teaspoon baking soda (the secret is in the soda — don't add too much!) and mix thoroughly. A chemical change will take place and the mixture will rise to a meringue-like consistency. Add a dash of salt, about a tablespoon of sugar to taste, a small amount of melted shortening, and enough flour to make a medium texture dough that will spread easily.

Force the dough into your awaiting oven; relax, and contemplate one of the great taste sensations in life. Sourdough, as everyone knows, also makes the best pancakes!

7. COOKING TRICKS

Figure 7-1

You'd think that culinary skill at home would translate to equal competence afield. Not always. That's because nature frequently doles out stoppers like rain, high winds, darkness, snow, crowded working conditions, canoe upsets, wet fire wood and unsafe water. Why rough it when, with a few tricks, meal preparation can be "smoothed" to a simple task? The following pages will show you how.

PACKING SUGGESTIONS

Scenario: It's twilight and misting when, after ten hours of hiking, you arrive at your wilderness base camp. Hastily, you pitch a rain tarp while friends see to the tents. First order of business is a rejuvenating supper of "Classy Spaghetti." Thoughts race through your mind as you search for the ingredients:

Hmmm ... got the spaghetti but where's the tomato paste? Ahhh, got it! "Hey, you guys, anybody seen the dried hamburger? Damitall, where's the Parmesan cheese?"

Last thing you need now is to search for things. *Everything* for the meal should be immediately at hand, all packed in one bag. This, you should have done at home!

To save weight and bulk, remove all unnecessary cardboard and paper packaging from foodstuffs *before* you go afield. Re- pack pre-measured amounts of "flowable solids" like sugar and Bisquick inside Zip-Lock bags. For added security against punctures, place each Zip-Lock into a color-coded cloth bag. A masking tape label will tell you what's inside. *Important:* don't forget to include the preparation directions with each entree or ingredient.

Breakable and crushable items like crackers, cheese, candy bars and fruit should be packed inside rigid cardboard containers or your coffee pot. I use cut-down half gallon milk cartons, which double as emergency fire-starters.

Liquids are best carried in plastic bottles that have screw caps. Genuine *Nalgene* bottles — available at most camping shops — are by far, the best. High grade plastic 1500 milliliter medical IV bottles, which contain "sterile water for irrigation," are also superb. Hospitals discard them after a single use. Ask your doctor to save some for you. Plastic bottles with pop-tops and flip-tops, like those which contain pancake syrup and cooking oil, usually leak. I melt these tops shut in the flame of a gas stove.

Food tubes are plastic tubes which open at the back so they can be filled with peanut butter, jam, etc. A questionably sturdy clip seals the contents. Use food tubes like toothpaste: remove the cap and squeeze. Sounds great, but these units frequently fail, usually in your pack. Always keep food tubes in Zip-Lock bags, "just in case."

Nalgene
bottle

1500 ml
IV bottle

Nalgene
bottle
with leash

Figure 7-2   Nalgene bottle and 1500 ml IV bottle.

When packaging each meal, fold over the sharp corners of foil packages so they won't cut through the adjacent plastic bags.

Tips

1.   Sorting meals will be easier if you package them in color-coded nylon bags. I use *green* for breakfasts, *blue* for lunches, and *red* for suppers. *Everything* for a given meal goes in the bag.

2.   Pack a few sheets of paper toweling with each meal to serve as dish towels. Toilet paper — the Boy Scouts call it "AP" (all purpose) paper — also makes acceptable toweling. Please burn or pack out used toweling and packaging.

FOOD PREPARATION IDEAS
HOW TO PREPARE FREEZE-DRIED FOODS SO THEY ALWAYS TASTE GOOD

Modern freeze-dried foods are marvelous *if they're correctly prepared*. And following the "package directions" is no guarantee for success. Indeed, what works at home often fails on a flat rock in a norwester. Here's a proven method that works no matter what the weather.

STEP ONE

Separate the component parts of the meal. Ordinarily there are three packets: pasta, meat, spices.

STEP TWO

Place *20 percent more water* into your cooking pot than is called for in the package directions. Add the contents of the meat packet to the *cold* water.

STEP THREE

Fire up your stove and place your *covered* pot on to boil. Add a dash of your special "all spice" (see page 28) to the meat and water.

STEP FOUR

When the water boils, add the contents of the *spice* packet, if there is one. Stir to mix, then let simmer five minutes.

STEP FIVE

--Add contents of pasta packet to the simmering mixture, and increase heat to boiling. Stir frequently until pasta is done. If you're short on stove fuel, use a one minute boil, then set the covered pot aside in a warm place for 15 minutes, to complete cooking. In cold weather, place a jacket or sweater over the pot to provide insulation.

That's it. Your meal is done. All portions are thoroughly cooked and the taste is fully developed.

WHY SOME MEALS FAIL

1.   You haven't cooked the meat long enough. Dried meats

require time to rehydrate, the reason why you should start them in cold water.

2. You burned the pasta — easy to do on a stove or campfire if you add everything at once. Pasta should always be added last — or for a class act, cooked separately.

3. Not enough water. I always increase suggested amounts by about 20 percent.

4. Insufficient spices. Use generous amounts of your all-spice and supplement with fresh or dried onions, celery and green peppers.

5. Spoilage: Aluminum foil is a complete oxygen barrier. Foods packed in vacuum-sealed aluminum theoretically have an unlimited shelf life (same as canning). Plastic-bagged foods, on the other hand, merely "inhibit" the passage of oxygen molecules. In time (shelf life is about a year), aerobic bacteria in the food will cause spoilage. So unless you plan to freeze them, don't buy foods in September for use the following July. Your autumn bargain may become summer indigestion.

MAKING POPCORN

If you're tired of trying to season popcorn in a pot that's too small, carry a large paper grocery sack on your next campout. Pour each batch of completed popcorn into the bag (don't use a plastic bag — hot corn will melt through it!) and season it there. Afterwards, burn the bag.

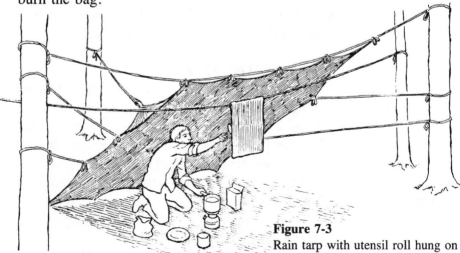

Figure 7-3
Rain tarp with utensil roll hung on tight line below.

COOKING IN THE RAIN

When rain threatens to spoil your stew, erect a 12' x 12' rain tarp and move the kitchen under it.* Rig a tight line just beneath the fly and snap your utensil roll to the overhead cord (figure 7-3) Now, everything from spices to spoons will be immediately available and protected from weather and the wet ground.

In summary, an ounce of re-packing at home is worth a pound of fumbling afield. Plan, pre-measure, and test new food ideas — and food containers — in the comfort of your kitchen, not in a remote bush camp where the price of failure is high. And don't rely on culinary skill to outfox the environment. Only a well-rigged rainfly will do that!

---

* See my books, *Camping Secrets,* or *Basic Essentials of Camping,* for the specifics of fly rigging and the knots and hitches needed to rig a snug camp.

8. ON INTO WINTER

Figure 8-1

It's mid-February and ten above in northern Minnesota — a glorious day for traveling.

"Looks like a blue wax day," calls Willie. *"Yeah,"* I mutter, and chalk one ski, fumble and drop the tube of wax into a four foot snow drift. I dig hard with my poles, and with grit determination, herringbone up the tortuous trail. Thirty minutes later I reach the top, flushed and sweating, my senses not yet attuned to the crisp solitude of the lake country's wintery white. I dream of camp, a roaring fire ... and Roger's chili.

54

I snap on my headlamp and peer at my watch: five p.m. and almost dark. The thermometer stands at twenty below.

The water in the big Sigg pot is near boiling, so I set the gallon milk carton of frozen chili into it. Soon the cardboard separates from its contents and I remove it from the pot.

"Hey Marc, I need more water!" "Poly bottles by the pulk," comes the reply. I pull one bottle from the snow and pour its contents into the steaming pot.

Twenty minutes later the chili boils, and as is the cook's prerogative, I try a spoon. Awful! It tastes like burnt peppermint.

"Hey, you guys," calls Marc. *"Anybody seen the peppermint Schnaaps?"*

As you can see, sub-zero temperatures, poor light, and downright carelessness, tend to complicate food preparation. Here are some ways to avoid the pitfalls of cooking in winter.

THE RIGHT FOODS

You burn a lot more calories in winter than in summer. So load up on carbohydrates and increase fat intake to 35-40 percent of your total calories. Fatty sausages like salami, Cervalot and pepperoni are ideal winter fare, but peanut butter (a summer favorite) is not. Try chiseling Peter Pan out of a poly bottle at 15 below and you'll see why!

Cheese, another nutritious high fat food, tastes like candle tallow when frozen. The solution is to thaw it in a parka pocket, or melt it into the evening's spaghetti.

FOOD PREPARATION TIPS

Low temperatures and an icy wind make even an efficient stove seem lazy. So burrow your kitchen deep into the snow, away from drafts. And bring *much more* stove fuel than you would in summer. A liter a day for a party of four is about right. Since a hot stove will melt its way down through a snowbank, be sure to provide a stable support. An inverted pie tin, plywood square, or piece of closed-cell foam works well. Don't set stoves on snowshoes or fiberglass pulk's (sleds): the heat may warp them.

COOKWARE

Select your plastic cups and bowls carefully. Plastics which are brittle in the store may shatter afield. Give your plastic cookware the "home freezer test" before you commit to them in frigid temperatures.

DISH WASHING

Bacteria are dormant in sub-freezing temperatures, so you need not wash dishes at all — that is, as long as you don't share eating utensils with your friends! A lot of winter campers simply wipe out their bowls with snow and go about their business.

Frankly, I prefer a more civilized approach. I "swirl and rinse" (no soap!) cookware in boiling water, then call it quits. To keep my hands toasty warm and dry, I wear light wool gloves inside plastic coated cotton ones.

FOOT LOOSE

"Standing around" at 20 below, waiting for a pot to boil, can be a chilling experience, even with good boots on. A square of half-inch thick closed-cell foam will take the edge off what's underfoot and double as a sitting pad in camp.

A BEAM INTO THE NIGHT

Meal preparation is necessarily complicated by the long winter nights which, in northern latitudes, may keep things blacked out for 12 hours or more. If you plan a pre-dawn start or late day finish, you'll need some sort of artificial light for cooking. Standard flashlights are inefficient in the cold, and candle lanterns don't put out enough light. Best, is a miner's headlamp — the kind that takes four D-cells. I use alkaline batteries and keep the battery pack warm inside my parka.

FROZEN LIQUIDS?

Freezing begins at the air interface of a liquid, so store your water bottles *upside down* in the snow. This way, you can forgo the difficulty (impossibility!) of removing frozen bottle caps.

Figure 8-2   Be careful around stoves when you're bundled up!

COOKING DANGERS

1. Be extremely careful around stoves when you're bundled up! Sub-zero clothing is a marvelous insulator. You may be fully afire and not know it till it's too late!

2. *Always* wear gloves when handling liquid stove fuels in sub-freezing weather. Liquid fuels freeze at much lower temperatures than water. Spill gas on your skin at 20 below and you'll suffer immediate frostbite!

LEFTOVER FOOD

In summer, you'd bury or pack out what you don't eat. In winter, there is no biological decomposition so you *must* pack out leftovers!

These are the basic cold weather cooking tricks. To this, add a love of wintery white, a generous measure of comraderie and a mixture of care and competence, and you'll enjoy the worst of times on the best of terms.

9. ETHICAL CONCERNS

Figure 9-1

Autumn mist in the backcountry. One last outing before the icy throes of winter — a final opportunity to camp and fish and to enjoy the good times that go with warm friendships, bountiful wilderness, and fire-brewed coffee served steaming hot on a frosty morning.

In the distance, snuggled in dense hardwoods is the campsite which you discovered more than a decade ago. Hauntingly beautiful, it is your "special" place.

Excitedly, you shoulder your pack and struggle through lush vegetation to the clearing above. The view from on top is spectacular, just like you remembered it.

Then you see it, the remains of thoughtless campers who preceded you — broken beer bottles, rusty cans, scraps of styrofoam and fly-infested fish remains. Suddenly, this place is no longer special. It is a trash heap, an insult to man and God. A gnawing pain grows upward from the pit of your stomach and surfaces as rage. The spell is broken!

Ultimately, your anger subsides and you put your thoughts in order. The slobs who preceded you occupied this spot for the same reasons as you — beauty and solitude. But unlike you, they had no feeling for the land, no knowledge of the proper way to treat it. Most likely, their actions were the result of ignorance rather than wanton disrespect.

Renewed interest in outdoor recreation has placed heavy demands on our wilderness areas. But simply sharing the backcountry with others will not ensure its survival. What will, is an understanding of ecological relationships and a commitment to ethical land use procedures. Please pass on these tenets — with commitment and vehemence — to all who will listen!

DISPOSAL OF HUMAN WASTE
AND FOOD/FISH REMAINS

Bury these under a four inch soil cover, *out of the main camping area*, and at least 100 feet from water. Shallow burial ensures rapid decomposition. If you have a lot of biodegradable waste, dig several cat holes to reduce the volume of waste in a given spot.

Do not scatter foodstuffs on the surface of the ground with the thought that "animals will eat it." They surely will! And they'll bring their friends, again and again, often becoming vicious if they haven't gotten their fill.

Some campers cache their food in a tree to keep it out of reach of determined black bears. This is a good idea providing you *don't* use the same tree as everyone else! Bears are creatures of habit; once fed at a certain spot, they'll be back for more. And they're very adept at getting food packs down from trees. If they can't smell your food, they won't get it. Just seal your food in plastic so there are no odors, then set it in the woods (or tree it, if you prefer), well out of the immediate campsite.

Remember too, that through classical conditioning, animals learn to associate certain containers with the presence of food. How else can you explain why bears bite open clothes packs and tin cans (no odor here)? For this reason, you should keep traditional food containers out-of-sight.

Fish remains should not be thrown into a lake or river under the guise that "fish or turtles will get 'em." Viscera breed bacteria (a health concern) which use up the oxygen for fish and aquatic life — the reason why you should always bury these products.

Note: Never throw biodegradables into out-houses or Forest Service box latrines. Bears will knock box latrines off their foundations to get at the food inside!

CANS, FOIL AND OTHER NON-BIODEGRADABLES

You brought 'em in, you pack 'em out. Standard procedure is to burn out tin cans, flatten them with a rock, then carry them home. In areas where fires are not permitted, cans may be burned out on your trail stove — a one minute process.

OTHER CONCERNS

Bathing and Washing: Swimming's fine, bathing is not, even if you use biodegradable soap. Remember, biodegradable products break down from bacterial action which lowers dissolved oxygen levels in the waterway. Please soap up on land and rinse via a bucket brigade. Then ... go swimming!

Cutting vegetation: It's unethical (and usually illegal) to cut green trees or branches. If you need a stick for roasting hot dogs, use a dead one!

Rain-proofing your tent: Please don't trench around your tent to provide guttering for surface water. Once erosion begins, it continues! Use a plastic groundcloth *inside* your tent to trap flowing ground water that gets in through floor seams.

Finally, please be sure your fire is *dead out* (feel it with your hand!) before you move on. If it's hot enough to burn your hand, it's hot enough to burn a forest!

WHERE TO GET SAFE WATER

Authorities advise you to boil, filter, or chemically treat all water taken from a questionable source — sound advice if you have the chemicals or equipment and the self-discipline to use them. I confess to laziness in this respect: invariably, I drink untreated water but I'm very careful where I take it. Here are the guidelines I follow:

1. Go well away from shore to get your drinking water. On a river, take your water *upstream* of the campsite.

2. Decay organisms generally prefer the shallows, so the deeper your water source, the better.

3. Avoid water that has a greenish color. This indicates the presence of algae, and accompanying microorganisms. And stay away from backwaters, stagnant areas, and beaver dams and lodges. Beavers are the favored host of the "Giardia" parasite.

WATER TREATMENT PROCEDURES

Most pathogens are killed instantly when water reaches boiling. When boiling is impractical, use a chemical tablet (available at most pharmacies) or one of the ingenious filtration units sold at camping shops. "Potable Aqua," "Globaline" or other iodine based chemicals are more reliable in cold or cloudy water than "Halazone" which releases chlorine. If you select a commercial filter, make sure the filter pore size is small enough to remove Giardia.

You can also use liquid chlorine bleach with 4-6 percent available chlorine to purify water. Use two drops of bleach per quart of clear water and four drops per quart of cold or cloudy water. Let the treated water stand 30 minutes before drinking, longer if it is cold or cloudy.

APPENDIX 1

TRAIL STOVES AND MAINTENANCE TIPS

The most practical trail stoves for cooking in the outdoors are not necessarily those that burn the hottest or are most expensive. Use these guidelines as a basis for stove selection.

1. *Stove stability* is important. Avoid stoves that threaten to topple your spaghetti with every stir of the spoon. Look for a low-to-the-ground profile.

2. Ease-of-starting: Some stoves come equipped with pumps for easier starting and more efficient use in cold weather. Stay away from stoves that require considerable pumping to start or maintain flame.

3. Wind susceptibility: First time you have to build a rock wall around your stove to keep it perking in wind, you'll understand the importance of a good windscreen. Avoid aluminum foil windscreens that interfere with the use of skillet handles.

4. *High heat output:* For winter cooking you need blowtorch performance. A winter stove should boil a quart of water (at sea level) in an uncovered pot in less than five minutes. If you want efficiency, stick with stoves that burn white gas or propane (if you can carry the heavy fuel tanks). The efficiency of butane is directly proportional to heat and altitude. In below freezing weather, butane stoves don't work at all. On mountain tops, because of the low air pressure, they work fine. The typical butane stove requires at least eight minutes to boil a quart of water at 70°F., at sea level. Kerosene stoves burn hot and are very safe (they can't explode). However, kerosene is oily and smelly — the reason why it's unpopular. But if you're traveling in Europe, where white gas is unavailable, kerosene is the logical choice.

5. *Simmering heat:* High heat output is great, but so is a low-simmering flame. Some of the best winter stoves (like the MSR X-GK) are not adjustable enough for gourmet cooking.

6. *Weight:* Some of the most reliable and versatile trail stoves are relatively heavy by packpacking standards. Examples include the Optimus 111B and 111 Hiker, the Phoenix Mountaineer, and the venerable Coleman twin burner.

7. *Ruggedness:* If a part looks weak, it probably is. If there's a plastic knob which can burn or break, it will. If there are components which may be lost, count on it. The best trail stoves are rugged, compact, and have no parts to break, burn, assemble or lose.

8. *Gasoline or multi-fuel?* Get a multi-fuel stove only if you need it. Multi-fuel stoves don't burn as hot as equivalent gas models and they are much more expensive.

STOVE MAINTENANCE TIPS

1. For greatest efficiency and trouble-free operation, use Coleman or Blazo fuel (it's naptha, not white gas) in your gasoline stove. These pre-filtered fuels burn clean and have extremely high heat output.

2. Don't fill gasoline stoves more than three-fourths full. You need air space to generate pressure.

3. Empty the fuel from your stove after each trip. And, *burn dry* what you can't pour out. Fuel left in stoves leaves varnishes which clog jets and filters — the major reason for stove failure!

4. Once a year (if you use your stove a lot) add a capful — no more — of Gumout Carburetor Cleaner to your stove along with a half tank of gas. Burn the stove dry. The Gumout will dissolve built-up varnishes.

5. Keep your stove in a fabric sack when it's not in use. This will prevent dust and debris from getting into the working parts.

6. Lubricate leather pump washers with high temperature gun oil. Avoid use of multi-purpose and vegetable oils which may break down and gum up valves.

APPENDIX 2

COMMON WEIGHTS AND USEFUL MEASUREMENTS

3 teaspoons = 1 Tablespoon

2 Tablespoons = 1 liquid ounce

16 Tablespoons = 1 cup

1 cup = 8 ounces

2 cups = 1 pint

4 cups = 1 quart

½ lb. margarine = 1 cup

1 lb. of granulated sugar = 2 cups 1 lb. of brown sugar = 3 cups.

1 cup chopped nuts = about ¼ lb.

64 marshmallows = 1 lb.

No. 10 can holds about 12 cups of water.

1 level full Sierra cup holds 1⅛ cups water.

1 standard sized plastic insulated cup hold 1⅓ cups water.

1 medium onion = 2 Tablespoons of minced dry onions.

1 Tablespoon of fresh herbs = ½ teaspoon of dried herbs, or
    ¼ teaspoon of dried, powdered herbs.

1 cup sour milk = 1 cup milk into which 1 Tablespoon vinegar
    has been stirred.

1 cup sour cream can be made by adding ⅓ cup butter,
    ⅔ cup milk, and 1 Tablespoon vinegar.

Index